Letters to Roger Blin

also by Jean Genet

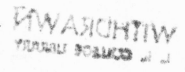

Letters
to Roger Blin

REFLECTIONS ON THE THEATER

by Jean Genet

Translated by Richard Seaver

GROVE PRESS, INC., NEW YORK

Photographs by Jacques Sassier

The Screens was first performed at the Théâtre de France on April 21, 1966, by the Jean-Louis Barrault—Madeleine Renaud Company. The sets and costumes were by André Acquart.

THE CHARACTERS*

(in order of appearance)

Saïd	*Amidou*
The Mother	*Maria Casarès*
Warda	*Madeleine Renaud*
Malika	*Annie Bertin*
The Maid	*Claudie Bourlon*
Mustapha	*André Batisse*
Ahmed	*Yan Davrey*
Brahim	*Victor Béniard*
Leila	*Paule Annen*
Sir Harold	*Paul Descombes*
Habib	*Jean-Pierre Granval*
Taleb	*François Hélie*

* This cast of 62 characters follows the Théâtre de France production. The play, as originally written and published, has a cast of 98 characters.—*Tr.*

Chigha	*Christiane Carpentier*
Kadidja	*Germaine Kerjean*
Nedjma	*Sylvie Moreau*
Habiba	*Micheline Uzan*
Si Slimane (Madani-The Mouth)	*Jean-Louis Barrault*
The Gendarme	*Jacques Alric*
Mr. Blankensee	*Régis Outin*
Malik	*Georges Sellier*
Abdil	*Michel Bringuier*
The Guard	*Robert Lombard*
The Lieutenant	*Gabriel Cattand*
The Sergeant	*Bernard Rousselet*
Pierre	*André Weber*
Roger	*Dominique Santarelli*
Jojo	*Michel Creton*
Preston	*Éric Gérard*
Walter	*Michel Lebret*
Hernandez	*Jean-Jacques Domenc*
Morales	*Michel Berger*
Felton	*Christian Jaulin*
Brandineschi	*Pierre Benedetti*
Mrs. Blankensee	*Marie-Hélène Dasté*
The Chief	*Jean-Guy Henneveux*
The Photographer	*Xavier Bellanger*
The Vamp	*Tania Torrens*
The Academician	*Michel Bertay*
The General	*Jean-Roger Tandou*
The Banker	*Jacques Alric*
The Communicant	*Brigitte Carva*
The Soldier	*Luis Masson*
The Man	*François Hélie*
The Woman	*Jeanne Martel*
Sir Harold's Son	*François Gabriel*
Salem	*Paul Descombes*

Naceur	*Pierre Gallon*
M'Barek	*Michel Dariel*
Lahussein	*Louis Frémont*
Srira	*Jean-Claude Amyl*
Larbi	*Patrice Chapelain-Midy*
First Combatant	*Christian Pailhé*
Second Combatant	*Christian Bujeau*
Amer	*Alain Hitier*
Abdesselem	*Guy Didier*
The Gendarme's Wife	*Catherine Rethi*
Djemila	*Michèle Oppenot*
Ommu	*Marcelle Ranson*
Nestor	*Luis Masson*
Lalla	*Jane Martel*
Aziza	*Céline Salles*
Aicha	*Marie-Claude Fuzier*

Letters to Roger Blin

My dear Roger,

Not all the living, nor all the dead, nor the generations yet unborn will be able to see *The Screens*. The whole of humanity will be deprived of it: there you have something that comes close to being an absolute. The world has managed to get along without them; it will continue to do so. Political nonchalance will allow a problematical meeting between a few thousand Parisians and the play. In order for this event—the performance or performances—without disturbing the order of the world, to impose thereon a poetic combustion, acting upon a few thousand Parisians, I should like it to be so strong and so dense that it will, by its implications and ramifications, illuminate the world of the dead*—billions of billions—and that of generations yet unborn (but this is less important).

I say this to you because the spectacle, so limited in time and space, seemingly intended for a handful of spectators, will be so serious that it will also be aimed at the dead. No one must be turned away from or deprived of the spectacle: it must be so beautiful that the dead are made beautiful too, and blush because of it. If you stage *The*

---

* Or, more properly, of death.

Screens, you must always work with the notion of a unique spectacle in mind, and carry it as far as you can. Everything should work together to break down whatever separates us from the dead. We must do everything possible toward creating the feeling that we have worked for them, and that we have succeeded.

Therefore the actors and actresses must be induced to put aside cleverness and to involve the most secret depths of their being; they must be made to accept difficult endeavors, admirable gestures which however have no relation to those they employ in their daily lives. If we maintain that life and the stage are opposites, it is because we strongly suspect that the stage is a site closely akin to death, a place where all liberties are possible. The actors' voices, moreover, will come only from the larynx: this is a difficult music to find. Their make-up will, by transforming them into "others," enable them to try any and every audacity: as they will be unencumbered by any social responsibility, they will assume another, with respect to another Order.

The costumes will not clothe them; stage costumes are a means of show, in every sense of the term. You understand, therefore, the beauty that must be theirs. Not a beauty of the streets but an essential beauty, the same as with the make-up and the altered voice, so that the actors can throw themselves into the adventure and emerge victorious from it. What we are talking about, therefore, is an accouterment. I should like the costumes of the three old ladies to be made of verminous and splendid rags. A few details here and there should remind one of Algeria, but the general style will be of great nobility: full, with trains and drapes, even if all this has dust and straw clinging to it. In a nutshell, each costume must be a setting in its own right—against a background of screens—capable of situating the character, but, once again, this sumptuousness must not derive from a wordly beauty, nor even from an imitated or parodied beauty, thanks to the old clothes; Acquart and his wife must be capable of inventing fright-ful accouterments, which would seem out of place on the shoulders of the living. Madmen, madwomen, Madwomen, are capable of sewing such costumes. I am sure that the Asylums are full of these ornaments, monuments, difficult to bear. The Mother, Kadidja, Ommu will be sheltered be-neath them, and, perhaps, will be slightly corrupted by them. But please, do not tolerate any prettiness. Acquart must almost be threatened. What a sorry lot the ordinary costumes in the theater! In them, the actors are afraid to try anything, they are condemned to mere pretty move-ments, either of the thighs, of arched feet, or of arms and torso.

Don't allow an actor to forget himself unless he carries this forgetfulness to the point of pissing squarely in front of the public. You should force them to dream—those who have no lines—to dream about the death of their son or the death of their beloved mother, or they should imagine that a thug is robbing them or that the public sees them naked.

The screens themselves: those that you and Acquart have made are quite beautiful. (I am referring to the way they are constructed and the way they move.)

But the drawings on them? This is going to be very dif-ficult. Here again we must think of the Spectacle. No pseudo-naive nonsense. The place to look is among the drawings done by madmen. Even among madmen who systematically feign Madness. Go spend a little time out at the Rodez Asylum. Buttonhole a nut, tell him this story about some other nuts, *The Screens*, and have him translate it into drawings. I believe that a sex maniac, who had never seen an orange tree in his life, nor even an orange, could invent a truer orange tree than anyone else. Where will we find him? Hold a competition? But if we *think* very hard about that, chance will work for us.

I come back to the actors' way of walking:

The Mother, with tiny steps, but the way she gestures bespeaks great authority. Then, suddenly, seven-league strides, with her skirt raised in such a way as to show her legs, the veins of which—blue or purple—will be visible.

Kadidja, haughty, her umbrella like a cane.

Ommu, pulling his foot, his paw, from the mire with every step. But the upper part of his body, from the chest up, very straight, his head straight, the flow of words cold and clearly articulated.

For Saïd, you see, the actor must learn to concentrate. One feels that he is not yet completely at ease either in Saïd's body or his manner of gesturing. For a few seconds, he has been known to wander off to Leopardi Square in Verona, or to the rue Saint-Benoit.

Warda presents a rather difficult problem: an extraordinary emptiness has more presence than the most dense fullness.

It's the Sergeant who bothers me: either it's you and your slightly wild and slightly bantering poetry, or it's the young man guided by you. I believe you will know how to turn him into the counterpart, luminous by Western standards, of Saïd; or, if you like, his opposite in all respects. Solar man as opposed to saturnine, even if the solar types give us a pain in the ass—and, in this case, it's we who will give them the pain in the ass. A good-looking wench in uniform.

People say that plays are generally supposed to have a meaning: not this one. It's a celebration whose elements are disparate, it is the celebration of nothing.

Leila I'm not sure about. Perhaps it's because she advances wearing a mask. I leave it to you to work out.

But as for the make-up, you must call upon your dreams, your daydreams, your wildest ravings, and not upon your reason, nor upon your observations unless they are mad and make you see a velvety fleece around the Arabs' eyes. Make-up intrigues me. It must remind one of, must call to mind, Algeria by methods of which the Algerians are unaware: I'm afraid of the henna tint for the Mother's hair. Algerian poverty and misery must have other colors and other materials, which must be discovered. You and Acquart have your work cut out for you. And I'm not making matters any easier.

And what is more, on stage a light so cruel! but that is what is required.

Let me come back to the actors: they are going to turn themselves into animals. We have to help them. With, from time to time, as they are performing, a bit of The Mother, or Ommu, or of Warda, who shows the tip of her ear. The rest of the time, animals. The way I read it—Nebuchadnezzar, grazing in the grass and, for a few minutes, king, and perhaps, a man.

The Mother: don't diminish her natural fury. Don't extinguish her fire, but add acting ability to it.

Kadidja is already the most important lady in the village: her umbrella will be bigger than the others.

Ommu, a full cut above: much higher than the most important lady of the village. Patronness of the revolt. And if the name means anything to you: Nemesis. In any case, supreme in this death which is taking place on earth.

Of course, everything I'm telling you, you already know. All I'm doing is trying to encourage you in your detachment from a theater which, when it turns its back on middle-class conventions, goes in search of its models: gestures, tone, in the visible life and not in the poetic life, that is, the one we sometimes find near the confines of death. There, faces are no longer ruddy, one no longer has the ability to open doors—or else it is a strange door indeed, opening upon what! In short, you really know what it is I should like to say, without finding the appropriate words.

And the ruin! I almost forgot the ruin! The ruin of the teeth cultivated with Warda's needle, and the total shambles of the play itself. I mean it: when the public leaves the theater I want it to carry the well-known taste of ashes and an odor of decay in its mouth. And yet I want the play to have the consistency of flint. Don't be afraid to have the actors and actresses transform themselves into jackals, turkeys, etc.—into trees too. I may seem to be uttering asininities, but you know very well what I mean. My play is dirty in that it does not contain the customary social crap, but it must be rinsed again with bluing.

What I also like is that, in order to underscore—or, if you like, lend special emphasis to—the stylization of the acting and diction, you occasionally find certain postures and tones of voice that are more realistic. It is in this vein that, at the point of the play where Warda is picking her gold teeth, one or two customers are combing their hair with a comb which has a number of teeth missing, their legs bent as though in front of a mirror. Of course all this has to be worked out.

I was a bit worried about the Lieutenant. But perhaps it was because I hadn't known what would suit him, that is, that instead of being a martinet pure and simple he should blow his stack and get into a violent argument either with the men or the Sergeant, or with the Captain, the way they say that the fishmongers of Marseilles blow their stacks, the chest thrust forward. I believe that at a certain point, I can't remember which, he must cease to be Susini and become a poor devil on the verge of losing control of himself.

The drawings. Let me say another word or two about the drawings on the screens: they ought to be eccentric, on a grandiose scale, but without disturbing the public. Where can we find that? When the orange grove is burning the flames must look like the foul flames a sadist would draw if he were asked to paint a burning whorehouse full of naked women.

I don't believe you should anticipate there being any more than four or five performances. Actually, if the actors and actresses delve deeply within themselves, they will not be able to hold out for very long. Or so it seems to me. Any performances beyond the first five will be reflections. In any case, such is my impression. And besides, what does it matter? A single performance properly staged ought to suffice.

We must be careful about the ceiling of the stage. Even if it serves no purpose—adds nothing to the acoustics, for example—white strings must be stretched from the public toward the rear of the stage. Normally, unless there is some kind of ceiling, it's always ugly.

* * *

Raise the proscenium arch (is that the proper term for it?), if you can, to the maximum height.

* * *

Madani-The Mouth's acting: he is always a trifle emphatic. Madani ought to display a touch of bombast, in the beginning, and the Mouth everyday irritation. But you and Jean-Louis Barrault will easily work out the difference between the tone of the Mouth and that of Si Slimane awake.

* * *

I see the dead as being heavily made-up—but with green the dominant color. White clothing, suggestive of winding sheets. Their diction will be different. It will be louder and closer to everyday language.

* * *

The dead soldiers could be wearing fatigues, rather loose fitting, with the wounds painted on with red paint.

* * *

I think that a single performance is enough, rather than five. But one polished and perfected over a period of six months.

* * *

Have Saïd stop rolling his eyes. And ask the actors, during the performance, not to let themselves slip back into the movements and gestures that are theirs off-stage, or that they resort to in other plays. It is normal for them to try and find the gestures that are suitable both to the character they are playing and to their own personality, and once they have found them let them keep to them. But in general they smugly do whatever strikes their fancy, in order to seem spontaneous!

* * *

I think that the living soldiers could wear the uniform of the Conquest (the type worn by the Duke of Aumale) and kick the bucket in the same uniform. The point of this being not to situate too precisely in time a play which is a masquerade.

* * *

It is impossible for the glory, solitary and solar, for the virtues of a man or a people to be reduced, first by analysis, to no more than a repository or a receptacle, that which remains of a man or a people when their embellishments have been stripped away, but the shame that remains, after a life of treason, or even after a single act of treason, is surer. Shame is less prone to being shaken than is glory. It will in fact never be shaken; on the contrary, time hardens and, in a way, restores it, luminous, more glorious than glory, inviolate.

A people solely distinguished by periods of glory or men of virtue would be inevitably subject to analysis and reduced to nothing, save a receptacle. The crimes of which a people is ashamed constitute its real history, and the same is true of a man.

* * *

I write that because, if you read it to the actors, they may know what I'm talking about.

* * *

What I'm talking about, of course, is theatrical conduct, and I have been at pains to indicate that the stage and life are opposites. My play is not the apologia for treason. It takes place in a realm where morality is replaced by the esthetics of the stage.

* * *

Time. I know nothing very specific about time, but, if I acknowledge the existence and termination of an event, any event whatsoever, it seems to me that the event did not take place in a movement going from the present moment toward the future, but that, on the contrary, the moment which is going to direct the event is no sooner born than the event culminates and flows back at top speed toward its birth, and settles upon itself. The first Frenchmen bombarding Algiers in 1830, if you like, bombarded themselves from Algiers about 1800. Events are thus born, spontaneously, and die at the same instant of the same movement, but die so quickly that their end, turning round, brings them back to a point slightly prior to the noise which marked their birth. They are as hard as pebbles. The French Revolution, in "my" story, has not yet come full cycle upon itself. The event which extends from 1789 to the present day is therefore somewhat nebulous, but within it the conquest and loss of Algeria is a compact entity.

I haven't the time to go into the matter at greater length in order to make you understand that the dead or dying soldiers in this play must wear the uniform of the Duke of Aumale and the Duke of Bugeaud. The same movement of time which deposits them in Algeria expels them back into the sea. Even if, by their speeches, we understand that they were living in 1958. That is unimportant. They were foolhardy.

These natives of Alsace-Lorraine and convicts disguised as conquerors ought to be wearing really handsome costumes. Think therefore of Zouaves in their braids, of spahis in their black satin capes, their golden sandals, etc. It is without a doubt the most florid Army of the Republic. Each soldier like a gravestone in the Père-Lachaise cemetery.

That's the way I see it. No sooner had Dey's fan stopped moving, no sooner had the first shot of the cannon sounded, than 800,000 French settlers in Algeria were already fabricating Tixier-Vignancour.* Everything was very rapid, rapid enough *to bring off an event* which has neither beginning nor end: global.

* * *

Warda must be a kind of Empress, shod in half-boots so heavy—of solid gold—that she can no longer bend over. You can carry her as far as is feasible. Make her wear an iron corset. With bolts.

* * *

These, my dear Roger, are the only notes I have, which I leave to you to accept or reject. With them, I send my regards.

Jean Genet

---

* A political leader, head of the extreme right-wing Alliance republicaine pour les libertés et le progrès. —*Tr.*

Daily Notes

Italian-style theater is not long for this world. I know nothing of its history, how it began nor why it culminated in a kind of well with dress circles, ground-floor boxes, first-tier boxes and top galleries (what names!),* but I feel it dying together with the society which came to see itself mirrored on-stage. This fulfillment corresponded to a fundamental immorality: for the poultry of the top galleries, the "house"—dress circle, orchestra, boxes—was an initial spectacle, which in essence formed a screen—or a prism—which their gaze had to pass through before perceiving the spectacle on-stage. The top galleries saw and heard, as it were, through the screen made up of the privileged public of the orchestra and box seats.

* * *

The spectators in the orchestra and boxes knew they were being looked at—greedily—by the public in the top

---

* Much of the flavor of the names of various kinds of theater seats is lost in translation. For example, the ground-floor boxes are called *baignoires* in French, which is also the word for "bathtub"; the galleries are called *poulaillers*, which also means "hen house" or "hen roost."—*Tr.*

galleries. Knowing themselves to be an entertainment before the show, they acted as an entertainment must: in order to be seen.

On one side as on the other—I mean upstairs as well as down—the performance on-stage never reached the public in a completely pure state.

And I am not forgetting the velvet or crystal, or the gold leaf whose purpose is to remind the privileged public that the theater is their domain, and that the play is demeaned and degraded proportionately as their distance from the main floor and the carpeting increases.

* * *

You will perhaps have theaters with ten thousand seats, probably resembling the Greek theaters, in which the public will be discreet and seated at random or according to their individual agility or on-the-spot ruse, not according to their rank or wealth. The play on-stage will address itself, therefore, to what is most naked and pure in the members of the audience. Whether the public's apparel is gaudy or sober, bejeweled or otherwise bedecked, it will in no way affect the integrity of the play being performed on-stage. On the contrary, it would be a good idea if a kind of madness, an effrontery, impelled the public to rig itself out in strange attire when it went to the theater—providing of course that it wore nothing blinding: brooches of undue length, swords, canes, mountain climber's pickaxes, lighted lamps in hats, tame magpies . . . or nothing deafening: the din of a drum-and-bugle call, transistor radios, firecrackers, etc., but that each person deck himself out as he wished in order to be receptive to the maximum degree to the play being performed on stage: the audience has the right to be mad. The more serious the play, the greater may be the audience's need to affront it adorned, and even masked.

One ought to be able to enter and leave during the performance, without bothering anyone. And remain standing too, and even walk up to the stage if one feels like it, the way one approaches a painting, or steps back away from it. Thus if *The Screens* were being performed at this period, a certain space would have to be reserved directly on-stage for a certain number of walk-ons—silent and motionless—who would be part of the audience, having donned costumes designed by the costume designer—the notables on one side of the stage, and the common-law convicts on the other, masked and in chains, guarded by armed gendarmes.

* * *

While I was writing this play, I pictured it as being performed in an open-air theater in which the tiers of seats, carved out of the side of a hill, would be mere earthen benches. The stage at the bottom of the hill, and the sets (the screens) standing out against the trees of a full-grown forest.

* * *

There should be added to the text of *The Screens* something approximating a score. This is within the realm of possibility. The director, taking into account the various tonal qualities of the different actors' voices, will have to invent a manner of speaking which ranges from murmurs to shouts. Sentences, a tempest of sentences, must be delivered like so many howls, others will be warbles, still others will be delivered in a normal conversational tone.

The director will decide what the Mother's barking noises should be—which will be very different from what Leila's should be. The same will hold true for Scene Fourteen. It will be the job of the actors on-stage to convey the thunder and the sound of the rain.

* * *

How will the drawings be done? The actors will have to be taught. Using colored chalk, they ought to achieve some really festive effects on the screens. Even the drawings of the mountains of Giant Cedars, or of the Big Dipper: everything ought to be painted with care, the aim being to move the audience. Even if the drawings are unskillful, awkward, naive, the actors ought to put as much effort and concentration into doing them as they put into their acting.

The clock drawn by Leila will be a very handsome model of a Louis XV or Louis XIV clock, or even rococo, full of scrolls, flowers, etc.

* * *

A good deal of black material will have to be used for the costumes, to set off the other colors. The "background" of this play is black. I wonder why?

* * *

The props: the wheelbarrow, cheese grater, bicycle, gloves, etc., will also be interpreted. Larger than life, made of stronger material (the cheese grater out of cast iron), heavier, in order to command attention successfully in a space as big as this stage. In certain places they may be encircled with a black line, or their shadow traced on the ground, or on one of the screens by an actor, etc. The reason for this being to lend the moment a certain density. In short, treat everything as a joke.

* * *

Each scene, and each section within a scene, must be perfected and played as rigorously and with as much discipline as if it were a short play, complete in itself. Without any smudges. And without there being the slightest suggestion that another scene, or section within a scene, is to follow those that have gone before.

* * *

In the twelfth scene, the Arabs ought to make their drawings very quickly; but some of them must dally, and even a chosen few come back—even twice or three times in succession—to the screen with their chalk and their charcoal to put a final touch, to emphasize a shadow, etc.

Another Letter to Roger Blin

This is how I see certain costumes and make-up.

The Mother—Her hair of tow. A white face, made up with ceruse, and very elaborate wrinkles—blue, mauve, purple—from the eyes to the temples, from the wings of the nose to the mouth and down around the chin; finally, the tendons of the neck made very prominent. Her hands as white as her head, and the wrinkles, or rather the veins, extremely visible. The same for her legs, up to her knees. As for her eyes, not too large and not too oriental.

The dress, which is very heavy, comes down to just below her feet, so that the Mother has to lift it slightly in order to walk. The dress is made of rags from various cloths, of a variety of forms and materials, in different shades of purple and mauve. The seams will be visible, the rags having been pieced together with a coarse white thread.

* * *

Kadidja—Her face purple, almost black. The color of Negroes' lips, more or less. Her wrinkles, which are numerous, will be white. I think they ought to start at the wings

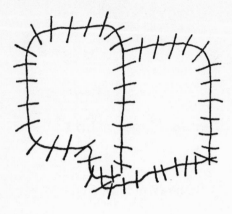

Of course, the drawings on the backs of the pages must be interpreted by you. You may well have different ideas about the dresses and make-up.

etc.

of the nose and move toward the hair, the ears, and the chin. Her hands, her lower arms, and her legs, made-up the same way.

She will use her black umbrella, sometimes closed, sometimes open, but patched together.

Her dress will be yellow. Every possible yellow, a patchwork of saffron, ocher, etc. Yellow even when she goes to mourn the dead. But it's a dress that can be raised belt high, over a long petticoat, dragging on the ground, perhaps of dark blue material. (Talk this over with Madame Acquart.)

White hair, but stiff, drawn back.

* * *

All the other women will have umbrellas and will be dressed in the same way, with skirts made out of yellow or greenish rags.

* * *

A suitcase full of gifts?

The consummate whore.

A whore ripens slowly.

Warda (Madeleine Renaud) about to be screwed by Saïd, who has saved up his money for her.

Leila has only Saïd's trousers. Instead of sewing them, she adores them.

Sir Harold is greatly amused at the idea that Saïd is going to leave his orange groves for Le Creusot.

Casarès and Annen about to feed the farm animals, the sounds of which they themselves provide.

How the family awaits a son whom prison has turned into a king.

Casarès, Amidou, and Paule Annen: Saïd has just got out of prison.

Casarès is decidedly the Mother, ready to confront the women of the
village and the theater audience.

(ABOVE) Kerjean and Casarès about to yell at each other: the Mother will not go to mourn the dead. (BELOW) Casarès doesn't give a damn either about the women of the village or the dead. She wants her glory.

Jean-Louis Barrault about to become the Mouth of Si Slimane.

Now Barrault is the Mouth of Si Slimane. He rejects Casarès from the world of the dead as Kerjean has rejected her from the living.

After the Mouth's intervention, Barrault demands his payment: coffee. He had to go into a trance to be the Mouth; the coffee brings him back among us.

Leila or Paule Annen, whichever you prefer, the thief of unusable objects.

Everything in the eye, or the metamorphosis into Fatima.

Your orange trees, your roses, your cork oaks— French beyond all shadow of a doubt—are impressive, before death or flight.

(ABOVE) Paulette Annen's despair.

(BELOW) From his prison, Saïd cries out his despair to Leila who, if she were not on the stage of a theater, would be in another prison.

(ABOVE) In the Lieutenant's reply, where he says: "Work on your necks by torsion, tension, fluction, etc.," the author forgot the word masturbation.

(BELOW) France.

Kerjean dead, but screaming her orders before she dies.

Ommu—White hair that falls down over her shoulders. She's the crazy one of the three. White hair, very white.

A dress made out of sacking; if you like, a kind of very rough gunny sack. Cut into an assemblage of pieces, like the others' dresses. But this time with a very full skirt and a sort of train that she will hold up with the hand she is not using to hold her cane. She is wearing shoes with very high heels. She has to be taller than Saïd.

Her face will be yellow, beset by an infinite number of small wrinkles in among the very large and very dark (brown) circular wrinkles which will make her face look like a full moon, if possible covered with craters and lunar seas like the Sea of Serenity. Get a photograph, very much enlarged, of the surface of the moon. Ask for one from the National Aeronautics and Space Administration. The same holds true for her legs and arms: holes and monticules.

* * *

Warda—Her face completely white. She is painted in the presence of the audience. I see her green. In a big white petticoat, not patched together from many different pieces but cut out of some good material, perhaps pink. A gilded greatcoat will be draped over her. Like a cope of the Blessed Sacrament. Heavy, gilded ankle-boots. If possible made out of cast iron. Her hair sky-blue. A chignon set very high on her head. Like the chignon Marie Antoinette wore before she went to prison. Very high. Full of hat pins. Gilded make-up, or something akin. Golden hands. Don't bother your head too much about Algeria.

Warda's teeth: false. Buck teeth with plenty of gold, like Saïd's. And like those that Leila will have.

* * *

I've forgotten the names of the other women, except that of the widow Germain. Her, you should sweeten up. She has two teeth left: one in the upper left part of her mouth, one in the lower right part. Her lips sunken. Work on her face, with diagonal wrinkles, in such a way as to form diamond shapes. Turn-of-the-century dress. Blond hair, with ringlets: as cute as can be.

* * *

Saïd—I'm tired. In any case, make his ears stick out even more, and his mouth more flabbergasted.

* * *

Make all the actors work. I have the impression that they think they can do anything. It's imperative that they be taken completely aback, in accordance with the meaning of the term as you see it.

All best,

Jean Genet

Actually, I think that we should look for make-up, and for gestures and movements to go with it, of a much more evil sort. I've really been far too timid.

Genet

Another Letter

This is the way, my dear Roger, I have seen the first part of the play.

> The following I have found admirable:
> What you have done
> Maria Casarès
> Paulette Annen
> Amidou
> Madeleine Renaud (very young, perfect)
> Jean-Louis Barrault
> Cattand
> Kerjean
> Weber
> Granval (he's made enormous strides)
> The couple who pins
> Alric
> Rousselet shows great promise.

There is very little one can tell them by way of direction. I think that they will find within themselves, as they rehearse, the means to perfect their roles.

This still leaves the others: let's not talk about them for the moment.

For the notable, find a kid eighteen years old, with a

squarely clipped white beard and artificially white hair. The young actor made up as an old man will have to fabricate attitudes of old age. Otherwise, it's hopeless.

A rule which in any event must not be broken:

The Man, the Woman, the attitude and the word which in real life seem abject, in the theater must fill the audience with wonder, without exception, must always astonish by their elegance and their obviousness.

Nothing on-stage, nothing that ought to be ugly or ridiculous, of course.

Perhaps you ought to take aside those whose names I have mentioned to you and make full use of them to enhance the play—and therefore themselves.

Try, in spite of everything, to lead them toward a more hieratical theater. Otherwise, ARSENIC.

Or hit them. I can't send you a team of wrestlers to wipe them out. But *they already are!*

Two pages of notes follow.

Notes

Saïd's first shout ends, or is uttered, as a statement. *It shouldn't be.* He ought to raise his voice and leave it suspended: Not Ro*se*! but *Ro*se!

* * *

He makes two or three gestures that are not voluntary, but submitted to. Gestures which sustain *quite naturally* the spoken word. These gestures lessen his verbal and gesticulatory impact.

* * *

When he lets his hands fall back onto his thighs we can hear it in the audience. This is disturbing. We should hear nothing at all when he claps his hands and strikes his thighs.

We should not hear anything, even when the crowd runs across the stage, especially not the sound of the floorboards.

Nor should we hear anything when the Mouth strikes the floor to call the dead—or else we should hear something else, an atomic explosion if you can manage it, I'd much prefer that.

* * *

37

When the Mouth answers the Mother, who asks him if it's time, Jean-Louis Barrault ought to fish out his wrist-watch and dangle it in her direction, but without looking at it himself.

* * *

Sir Harold's son ought not to lower his head when he tells his father "yes" (in response to his father's question about whether he is armed), but raise it.

* * *

In the scene of the dead, when the Mother upbraids the women, I wonder whether she ought not to clench her fists as she stretches them out, rather than hold them open.

Open hands are more the symbol of entreaty. In any case, since she does it twice, I think she ought to have her hands open at first, then clenched the second time.

* * *

In prison:
Remove the Voice once and for all. The text is too flat.

* * *

My purpose in writing this passage was to recreate the prison. I haven't succeeded in finding the proper tone.

* * *

Leila should greet the Gendarme before her line: "I'm Saïd's wife." First the curtsy.

* * *

The yapping of the two women, mother and daughter, very pretty, but when she comes, before barking in support of her mother, Leila must smell her out: then yap with her. Then against her, etc.

* * *

Maria Casarès hasn't learned how to rest in the paroxysm: she's going to be exhausted. But she is so beautiful in her exhaustion!

* * *

Very good, the Mouth's differences of tone. His voice suddenly fresh and young when he answers as Slimane. But be careful about his age; sometimes, before his fatigue, or feigned fatigue, the deep voice returns. If Jean-Louis Barrault can rid himself entirely of his Parisian tone of voice, in the role of Slimane, he would be magnificent.

* * *

The Mother does not hunt for the gravestone with a sufficient display of myopia. She ought to make a greater show of making out the names on the graves.

* * *

You've cut the story about the cork oak trees and the sawdust corks. Why? I was rather fond of it.

* * *

The two colonists, seated, ought to be back to back, not side by side.

* * *

Kadidja (Kerjean), dead, issuing instructions for washing her own body.

Everything's going to rack and ruin.

(ABOVE) Leila knows how to do everything: the dog, the cock, the chickens, and even shoot the breeze with Madame.

(BELOW) You see, paratroopers can only walk now in a squatting position. Their stature is already a foul posture.

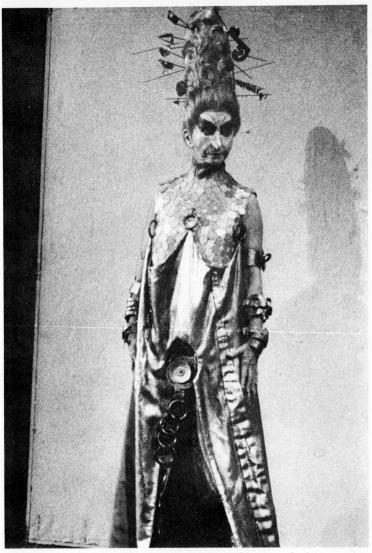

Slaughter is called for. Warda has split herself in two, the better to . . .

(TOP LEFT) Weber lost in the Moslem night with his Lieutenant's glass of water.

(MIDDLE AND BOTTOM) How the Mother, without even seeming to lay a hand on him, can get a soldier of the Foreign Legion all twisted up . . . and strangle him.

Malika is perhaps going to force the revolutionary to ask himself some questions.

(ABOVE) Cattand—or how a Lieutenant dies out of love. (BELOW) Tandou—or how a General dies under the mocking gaze of Cattand.

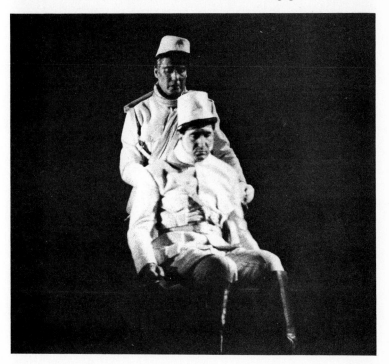

Ommu takes up the vigil.

A whore who has gone to school in Europe.

The Mother is about to arrive.

She is there at last, in all her glory.

The Lieutenant really dies.

Immediately after death, can gaiety be possible?

You have before you the danced song of Paule Annen's death.

(TOP RIGHT) Not quite dead, Warda arrives in the region of the dead.
(MIDDLE) And here is the Sergeant already dead, and dying shitting his death between Casarès and Renaud.
(BOTTOM) "Everything's going to rack and ruin," says the author of the play.

Ommu about to sing the praises of evil.

The stage of the Théâtre de France on a night of dress rehearsal.

Saïd about to sell himself to the highest bidder: the Revolution or the informer.

Words fail me when it comes to commenting on Saïd's murder.

The two preceding pages are some suggestions offered with a view toward rectifying, but the play taken as a whole is astonishing. That you have understood the play as I desired is not surprising, for you are quick to understand and discriminating, but you have had the talent and tenacity to apply your understanding. I would have liked to dissociate myself from this performance: I no longer have the strength to do so. Your spiderlike patience and the degree to which you have succeeded have ensnared me in your web. The job done by the actors and actresses whose names I have mentioned, under your direction, I consider as a personal tribute. I am happy, and a trifle ashamed at being so.

In *The Blacks*, the text of which was more carefully prepared as to its effect, your work amazed me less. In any case, it seems to me that I was as much responsible for its success as were you. In *The Screens*, the full credit goes to you. If I had thought that the play could be performed, I would have made it more beautiful—or a complete failure. Without touching it, you have taken it and made it light. It's very beautiful. You have my friendship, and my admiration.

Jean

There are still many things that need to be said, but they slip my mind.

You and Barrault must have cut a great deal. It seemed to me a trifle skimpy. You mustn't be afraid to breathe, and to know that we have a whole life ahead of us in which to put on this play. The audience will follow what you have done quite naturally. If it is well done, you won't bore anyone.

Another Letter with Notes

Dear Roger,
 Another couple of notes.

*   *   *

The Gendarme's explosion is not violent enough. After the exchange of the *"tu's"* and *"vous's"* there ought to be a slight calm, and a silence, then, without any warning, the mad explosion of the Gendarme, frothing at the mouth, driveling, etc. But in general he is perfect.

*   *   *

For each Arab soldier who is going to draw, you should invent a manner of walking which is constantly new: one walks forward with his hands in his pockets, lightly brushing the screens as he sways back and forth; another is full of determination; still another dragging one foot behind him; another dancing the java and having a good time, etc., and always Kadidja, motionless, never looking at the soldiers when she summons them, since she is dead.

*   *   *

Give Sir Harold some directions: he is caught red-handed. It is possible that he gets out of the difficulty.

* * *

Too frequently the actors look out at the audience. I think they ought to look at it without seeing it. In any case, when they do look out at the audience, they are wrong to look constantly at the orchestra seats. If, God forbid, they really feel compelled to look at it, then let them take the meaningful step of casting their eyes all the way up to the top galleries.

* * *

When Saïd alludes to the purchase of Leila from her father, he can chant his lines a little more than he does. A pretense of foolishness can help him to appear meaner.

* * *

Try to shift, to unbalance to some degree, the voice and acting of the woman mourner who talks for such a long time with the Mother (I don't know her name). Make her stutter, and see how that works. Have her bring her voice down two or three tones. She is too sober, too composed. Too good.

* * *

Work on the *Theft* (the scene preceding Saïd's release from prison). Too distinguished a theft. I would like it to be a little Neapolitan.

* * *

That seems to be all I have to suggest. What you have done is magnificent.

All best,

Jean

When the actors walk, run, jump through the doors or windows, they—or most of them—sound like a herd of elephants. Without creating the perceptible silence of nocturnal burglars, or of ladies who stoop down to peek through keyholes at their maids, I should like the actors to make no sound with their feet in order to replace it, if I may suggest, by a ringing sound similar to that made by my cane one day in Maria Casarès' living room when it struck the slender leg of a metal table. Therefore, silence to start with, in order to enable me to invent unexpected noises.

In the same way, don't let the Arab worker light a cigarette: the match flame not being able to be *imitated* on stage; a lighted match, in the audience or elsewhere, is the same as on-stage. To be avoided.

*   *   *

There are times when certain actors remain on-stage too long. One of the few expressions of theatrical jargon that I've remembered—but remembered clearly—is this: they are hamming it up.

The actor must act quickly, even in his slowness, but

his speed, lightninglike, will amaze. That and his acting will make him so beautiful that, when he is snatched up by the emptiness of the wings, the audience will experience a feeling of sadness, a kind of regret: they will have seen a meteor loom into view and pass by. This kind of acting will give life to the actor and to the play.

Therefore: appear, shine, and, as it were, die.

* * *

At first no one knows anything. The actors have little knowledge, but the man who is teaching them must know nothing and learn everything, about himself and his art, as he teaches them. It will be a discovery for them but also for him.

* * *

It seems to me that the public does not know how to listen. It tends to confuse two words: one hears with both one's ears, but one listens—or strains one's ears—with one's toes.

* * *

If I wanted the stage bathed in bright light, it was to keep each actor from covering up his errors, his fleeting mistakes, his fatigue, or his indifference, in a redeeming darkness. Of course, this much light will hurt him, but to be so brightly lighted will perhaps compel him.

* * *

While on the subject of lighting: it will be a good idea if each actor, by his performance, casts light on the other or others who, in turn, will cast their light on him. The stage will therefore be a site not where reflections spend themselves but where bursts of light meet and collide. It would by the same token be a site where Christian charity amused itself.

Notes Sent to Roger Blin
on April 14

Don't forget! All the make-up extremely violent, but all *asymetrical*.

* * *

For the young man who draws the revolvers on the screen: he must roll his sleeve up to his elbow, step back from the screen, so that only his hand and arm that are drawing are visible against the screen. The hand very heavily made up, so as to be visible.

* * *

The second young man: he will draw with short, angry strokes, doing an equally angry dance directly in front of the screen.—The heart to be drawn: it is the Sacred Heart of Jesus, with flames in place of the aorta.—Use surgeon's gloves, made-up: a make-up of black gloves and red blood.

* * *

Do the entrance of the Paratroopers over again: the first time, with the Lieutenant:

51

The Eucharastic Host and Latin, etc.
at one point the Lieutenant must turn around with a worried air, and the other Paratroopers must follow suit; they are walking backward, stooped over, afraid of the night.

* * *

The Arabs who draw:
    the first one stands behind Kadidja and holds out his open hands in front of himself and in front of her (he says he is holding revolvers);
    after he has raised his right sleeve, he begins to draw with rapid strokes.
    He steps back from his drawing the way a real painter would.

* * *

The Arab who draws the horns dances with a swaying motion over next to Kadidja, his hands behind his back.
    They must all be happy.

* * *

Ommu's performance:
    She overpoeticizes. You know what I mean.
    She ought to be less declamatory when she delivers the line where I say something to the effect: "It's the useless ideas that have to be protected and provoke song." This should be said very softly. While she runs.

When she wants her aspirin:
"My as——pirin!"
the way an addict calls for his heroin.

Notes Sent to Roger Blin
on April 15

Immediately replace the screen depicting the orange trees by a bare screen of one color, the dark blue of night, on which the Arabs will draw very vivid flames.

* * *

Think about suggesting to the Arab soldiers, at the very end, that before they fire at Saïd they ought to stoop down and look for him beneath the stage doors and windows as though they were looking in a thicket.

* * *

If Ommu uses crutches, it would be a good idea to cover them with bright red velvet, in tatters, and for Ommu to use them like knitting needles, as though she were knitting on the ground.

* * *

For Ommu: have her deliver her line at the end with impatience: "It's the unimportant things that have to live."

The quote is approximate, since I don't have the text. She must say the line with impatience, anger, clarity, irritation. Not the pompous way Merleau-Ponty would have said it.

* * *

A slightly faster pace for Sir Harold and Blankensee.

Another Letter

My dear Roger,

Since we are in agreement on this point—that the twenty performances which have already taken place* constitute only an approach of the play, or, if you like, a series of rehearsals—it is imperative that we review what works and what does not.

About the actors' performances: do I have to repeat myself? Saturday night, Maria [Casarès] was dazzling. I'm fully aware that it isn't, and will not be, Saturday every day, but she should be encouraged to maintain that brilliance. That evening she was a great tragic actress. Paulette is still working on her part, and will continue to do so; leave her alone. Barrault projected a tone that was moving, and gave a performance he ought to repeat in September. Even if in the beginning he was groping, the four or five last evenings he played Madani and Si Slimane superbly. Above all, let him maintain this attitude which is not absolutely safe.

---

* The first twenty performances of *The Screens* were given at the Théâtre de France in the spring of 1966. After the customary summer break, further performances were given during the fall. The present undated letter was obviously written immediately after the last performance given in the spring.—*Tr.*

That's it: it is imperative that no one have an attitude, or a series of gestures, which are perfectly safe. Barrault is constantly unstable, fragile, and unbreakable. I should like him too, like Casarès, Madeleine Renaud, and Kerjean, to be an example of strength and delicacy. An example, too, of theatrical meticulosity: he knows how to make-up his fingers and toes, and he takes the time to do it. Some evening take Amidou into Barrault's dressing room without any advance warning when he's making up his hands. For Madeleine—Barrault is right—we need a wig in disarray for the gunfire in the whorehouse. And let her play the perspiring baker's wife who's selling her bread like hot cakes.

But! What does not work? I can't say I'm pleased with the screens. If Acquart doesn't get bloody mad, we're done for. For the first screen: it's a tall palm tree, on a white or blue background, that has to be made to move. And all the others will be redone. Make it very clear to Acquart that the first problem is to understand what a screen is, and only then to decorate it.

Madame Acquart has made superb costumes, but for Christ's sake why is Alric dressed in hand-me-downs? And what about the soldiers? Michel Creton was right when he said to me: "We ought to be sexy too." The soldiers ought to have costumes cut and decorated like the Sergeant's, if you agree with the basic premise of wanting an already handsome Sergeant to be even more impressive. As for his acting (the Sergeant's), I was wrong to tell him to smile as soon as he made his first appearance on-stage. In the first part, before he breaks the screen of the dead, he ought to be a mean son of a bitch.

Each soldier will have, in addition to his accouterments and make-up, an attitude which is his alone, a made-up attitude, which will not be the same for everyone. You have to show it to them. No pockets on the knees. The Lieutenant will be far more dazzling if he is in charge of dazzling troops. Therefore, sexy soldiers, not rank rookies in fatigues.

Weber has succeeded in finding a very pretty make-up. So has Creton. But what about the others? You ought to draw it for them.

That's not all. Madame Acquart must remake Djemila's costume. (You can see that I'm making notes as the random thoughts occur to me.)

When the General rolls down the depths of time, have him pivot slowly, then faster and faster, the way a stone falls faster and faster, until the final impact, attaining, if he can, the speed of light.

The little drawing boxes—or pistols, as the utensils into which the weak and infirm piss are called—are very ugly. And what is worse, these pistols restrict the actors from making the gestures we would like: ample. Can't Acquart find another technique? The actors looked as though they were pissing off the stump of their forearm.

The idea of silken flames that rise and descend is very nice, but not out of orange trees that look like strawberry bushes. Against a background of night. Strawberry bushes!

Yes indeed, even if I'm satisfied, Rousselet has some more work cut out for him: more nervy, more of a bastard, and when he breaks through the screen he will have at last, on his coolly trained eye, his crown of periwinkles on his crossed eye. When he gives his account of his death, let him take his time. The public will listen.

And the farts? I refuse to give them up. Have you given up farting?

An important point: when Alric, well-dressed this time, does his belly dance, he ought to back off the stage, with his face to the audience, into the wing opposite from that into which Leila escaped flat on her belly. The public will not be fazed, even if it misunderstands; and, to take an example, let the Gendarme get lost on a false lead.

Cattand tends to look out at the audience too much. He also ought to address his soldiers, or stare into space, or do anything that crosses his mind. But nothing else in the way he acts should be changed, for it is all perfect. And I might add: perfect at the right time.

I'm getting to the point: you must make Marcelle Ranson work. She's ready and willing. She must have crutches with narrow strips of purple velvet wrapped around them. I really insist on this. Have her modulate the text more than she does. She'll know how to do it, but damn it, have someone work with her!

There are too many laughs in this play. Many ought to be silent, simply the soldiers' grinning faces. Or whistles. I leave it up to you to find the appropriate moments. You can very easily have the men and women whistle rather than laugh wholeheartedly. And what about the orchestration of laughter which I spoke to you about?

The Mother's farmyard is not varied enough: let the others help Maria and Paulette. The young actors could crow like roosters in the wings.

Another detail: when Saïd reappears on-stage, he will be wearing a new costume, made of purple rags.

* * *

Madeleine Renaud will come on-stage in the second scene from the wings, borne on the first step of a stepladder, and when Saïd—who will be invisible to the audience—arrives, she, clothed in the bishop's mantel, will ascend to the fourth or fifth step, and then finally to the top of the stepladder and, perched in this manner, she will leave the stage at the same time as the screen depicting the whorehouse from which the Arabs, who have just come and are fully satisfied, will emerge.

The dressmaker's dummy on which Warda's coat is draped is extremely ugly, to my mind. Acquart ought to make a new one.

* * *

The Arabs' quaking in the presence of Sir Harold's son: you need to work on this some more. Every actor must practice making all his limbs tremble in such a way that they all provide a painful vision of fear. They will tremble from head to toe, from their shoulders to their hands, and the trembling should be carried to trancelike lengths but should, in passing, evoke the image of a field of rye swayed by a strong wind, or the flight of a flock of partridges. Does that mean anything to you?

* * *

The actors playing the roles of Arabs could, if they are not too lazy, do something clever with their hair, either curl it, or put some kind of oily hair tonic on it, or some sticky substance, etc. There are many ways to make adolescent hairdos expressive, but, damn it, are these kids going to agree to work in front of a mirror not as gigolos but as actors?

* * *

The few demonstrators of the Occident group—* "In the deserted Occident what became of my boredom . . ."—give in to the lazy side of their nature when they see on-stage a dead French officer sniffing the meticulous farts of his soldiers, whereas they ought to be seeing actors playing at being or at seeming. . . . Actors' acting is to military reality what smoke bombs are to the reality of napalm.

* * *

They're the ones who are the real corrupters of the army, for if they read the word "chancre" in the dictionary they cannot help seeing chancres sprouting on all the military pricks transmitting chancres to all the tricolor asses. Now, they have read only seven letters, and because of them off they go to war. What a worrisome West!

* * *

This may not be an original thought with me, but let me restate it anyway, that the patron saint of actors is Tiresias, because of his dual nature. Legend has it that he retained the male sex for seven years, and for seven more the other. For seven years a man's clothing, for seven a woman's. In a certain way, at certain moments—or perhaps always—his femininity followed in close pursuit of his virility, the one

---

* Performances were interrupted on two occasions. The incidents were caused by a group of some fifteen or so first-year cadets from the French Military Academy of St.-Cyr. The first evening degenerated into a general riot, and on the second, sixteen members of the audience were arrested, but the play finally continued. Later, the Public Relations Committee of the Indochinese and Algerian Ex-Servicemen's League issued a proclamation calling on the people of Paris to stage a demonstration and to demand that *The Screens* be banned.—*Tr.*

or the other being constantly asserted, with the result that he never had any rest, I mean any specific place where he could rest. Like him, the actors are neither this nor that, and they must be aware that they are a presence constantly beset by femininity or its opposite, but ready to play to the point of abasement that which, be it virility or its opposite, is in any case predetermined.

Saint Tiresias, the patron saint of actors.

As for the divinatory powers of the saint, let every actor make an effort to see clearly within himself.

* * *

Of course I am completely ignorant when it comes to the theater in general, but I do know enough about my own.

Whenever a judge passes a sentence, let us demand that he be prepared other than by knowledge of the criminal code. Vigils, fasting, prayer, an attempted suicide or murder, could all contribute to making the sentence he is going to pass an event so momentous—I mean a poetic event—that he, the judge, having rendered it, will be completely exhausted, on the verge of rendering his soul either unto death or madness. Bloodless, voiceless, he would take two or three years to recover. This is a great deal to ask of a judge. But what about us? We are still a long way from the poetic act. All of us—you, me, the actors—must steep ourselves for a long time in the shadows, we must work until we are utterly worn out, so that one evening we come to the brink of the final act. And we must make many mistakes, and profit from them. The fact is that we still have a long way to go, and for this play neither madness nor death seems to me to be the fairest sanction. And yet it is these twin goddesses that we must move in order that they may turn their attention to us. No, we are in no danger of death, nor has poetry come the way it should.

If I wanted what you had promised me, bright lights, it was so that each actor would *finish* his gestures or lines brilliantly and would rival the brightest of lights. I also wanted the house lights to be on: with the collective ass of the audience scrunched down in its seats, its immobility imposed by the acting—that was enough to make a distinction between the stage and that house, but the lights are necessary for complicity to be established. A poetic act, not a spectacle, even were it beautiful in the normal sense of the term, would have taken place. Only Maria Casarès, because of her own innate ability, performed brilliantly the last evening.

In another letter, which you have probably lost, I told you that my books, like my plays, were written against myself. You know what I mean. Among other things, this: the soldier scenes are meant to exalt—and I mean *exalt*—the Army's prime, its chief, virtue: stupidity. Real paratroopers have given me a hard-on; I've never had an erection over stage paratroopers. And if I do not succeed through the text itself to expose myself, then you have to help me. Against myself, against ourselves, whenever these performances put us on God knows what decent side into which poetry fails to penetrate.

We have to consider that we have failed. Our fault lies in having lost our nerve, collapsing like a bagpipe which deflates as it emits a few sounds that we would like to think are attractive, and in our yielding to the illusion that the finished melody was well worth the loss of precious air. By small, successive stages we have slowly but surely turned the play into something insipid. Successive stages in order to make certain we would have a success which, to my mind, is in the final analysis a failure.

Jacques Maglia said to me: "Everything takes place as though the two of you, Blin and yourself, were proud as peacocks. Instead of a play which should stagger you when it is over, its seeming success reassures you."

I surrendered on several occasions to Barrault's objections, and to your own. Your knowledge of the theater threatens to make you avoid any errors of taste; my ignorance of this same profession should have led me toward them.

I am not maintaining that the *written* text of the play is of any great value, but I can assure you that I did not, for example, look down on any of my characters—be it Sir Harold, the Gendarme, or the Paratroopers. You can be sure that I have never tried to "understand" them, but, having created them, on paper and for the stage, I do not want to deny them. What binds me to them is something other than irony or contempt. They also help to shape me. I have never copied life—an event or a man, the Algerian War or colonialists—but life has, quite naturally, caused various images to come to life within me, or has illuminated them if they were already there—images which I have translated either by a character or an act. Pascal Monod, one of the students of the military, said to me after the last performance that the Army is not as much of a caricature as I have made it out. I did not have time then to answer him that what we are dealing with here is a dream army, a dream roughly sketched out on paper and, poorly or well, brought to fruition on a stage, which might be wooden and whose flooring creaks beneath one's footsteps.

Let us come back to the lighting. I'm sure you clearly understand that this way of playing with darkness, semidarkness, and light is a recourse, delightful and chilly, which gives the spectator the time to go into raptures or to regain his composure. I wanted the ice floe, the promised land which blinds and is unremitting. What ever happened to that white, metallic material that Acquart once talked to us about and which, according to my instructions, should have constituted the very material wherein the actors moved and had their being? Will it be possible for you to use this mysterious, Mallarméan, and allegorical material, even if only for a single evening's performance?

People don't go off to wage war if they don't love it, if they don't feel themselves made for—or, if you wish, destined for—combat. The same holds true for the theater. The actors, too much at ease on-stage, relax between their brief appearances, or, rather, crowd against one another around the blaring television in the actors' dressing room. Certain canons read their breviaries at vespers while their minds are a thousand miles away preoccupied with God knows what, but twenty-year-old actors should not be canons. Even when she is off-stage, Maria Casarès remains in the wings, attentive or exhausted, but present: the others get the hell away as fast as they can. They could at least have the courtesy to listen to what their fellow actors are saying on-stage. By dialing some buttons they tune out the voices coming from the stage, bearing with them bravura or weariness, failure or cleverness, and they are watching television. They are listening to it. Instead of leaving the world, they bring it back, as though the stage were a place of perdition. Young actors are remarkable in that they are no sooner on-stage than they do all in their power to conceal themselves, to dissolve into a grisaille of words and movements. Can't you tell them that to glitter too brightly in their daily lives off-stage prevents a long contained brilliance from exploding and illuminating the stage? Even if they have only one line to deliver, one gesture to make, that line and gesture ought to contain whatever luminous quality each actor bears within himself which has been waiting for a long time for this magic moment: to be on-stage. Surely every actor must be encouraged to be—were it only for the duration of a single appearance, lightning-like and true—of such beauty that his disappearance into the wings will literally break the audience's heart. And that the public, though it remains under the spell of what succeeds his exit, will still miss him after he is gone.

Finally, if I am so insistent about the bright lights, both the stage and house lights, it is because I should in some way like both actors and audience to be caught up in the same illumination, and for there to be no place for them to hide, or even half-hide.

These are the few notes, my dear Roger, that the production of *The Screens* and my friendship for you compelled me to make.

J. G.

Final Letter

I wrote to Maria Casarès to tell her more or less the following: "When you are explaining the situation to Saïd: 'You take the least expensive . . . you and she take each other, etc.,' I think that you should try these gestures: with each of your hands raised on either side of your face, and not supported by your knees, form a circle with your thumb and forefinger, more or less the way a lecturer does.

"And then, at the line: 'You take each other . . .' make both your hands point in one direction, away from Saïd."

If I am recalling this direction, it is so that you will better understand why, when we first started rehearsals, I forbade anyone to make the slightest gesture, however simple, with their body or their little finger. It seemed to me indispensable that the actors' voice expressed first, and by itself, as a notion of its body, the entire character. The fact is that actors are always prone to "finding spontaneously" gestures which help the words to emerge from the mouth. This— gestures and voice used in a banal way (according to the basic meaning of "banal")—results in a kind of useless redundancy. It is preferable, when the voice has found its true inflections, to discover the gestures which will then reinforce it, gestures which will no longer be familiarly granted the voice but will, perhaps, be in opposition to it —for example, to an inflection of deep regret a very light-hearted gesture of the hand and foot—in such a way that the whole forms a long succession of unstipulated agreements—broken but always harmonious, freeing the actor from the temptation of the commonplace.

This procedure, a refusal of a natural sham, must not be carried out haphazardly: its goal, among other things, is to reveal and make heard what *generally* passes unperceived. Its real goal, of course, is a new joy, a new festivity, and God knows what besides.

We were therefore lucky that a flamboyant temperament agreed to give this method a try. I was very much afraid of hurting Maria Casarès when I asked her, for example, to look at herself in a mirror, to make faces in it without indulgence, and to discover, in this new uglified face, a beauty that every spectator—not the public, but every spectator—could find within himself in some faltering way, buried but capable of rising to its own surface.

Perhaps by other means, without erasing the famous actress, and perhaps aided by you, but in any case with a great deal of courage, Maria has attained her and my own goal.

If this short book opens with your name, you will surely understand that I wanted to close it with the name of this admirable woman, who has constantly helped you with her Iberian fire and passion: Maria Casarès.

Jean Genet